GUIDELINES

Guidelines for Leading Your Congregation
Resource List

9781426736810	Set of 26 Booklets with CD-ROM & Slipcase
9781426736827	CD-ROM only
9781426736803	Set of 26 Booklets only
9781426736445	Adult Ministries
9781426736315	Advocates for Inclusiveness
9781426736438	Children's Ministries
9781426736421	Christian Education
9781426736261	Church Council
9781426736353	Church Historian
9781426736759	Church & Society
9781426736346	Communications
9781426736407	Evangelism
9781426736681	Family Ministries
9781426736377	Finance
9781426736773	Higher Education & Campus Ministry
9781426736285	Lay Leader/Lay Member
9781426736735	Men's Ministries
9781426736667	Ministries with Young People
9781426736414	Mission
9781426736308	Nominations & Leadership Development
9781426736278	Pastor
9781426736322	Pastor–Parish Relations
9781426736704	Scouting & Civic Youth-Serving Ministry
9781426736339	Small Group Ministries
9781426736216	Small Membership Church
9781426736391	Stewardship
9781426736360	Trustees
9781426736711	Women's Ministries
9781426736384	Worship

GUIDELINES

church
historian

*Remembering the Past
and Inspiring the Future*

The General Commission
on Archives and History

CHURCH HISTORIAN

Copyright © 2012 by Cokesbury

This book is printed on acid-free paper.

ISBN 978-1-426-73635-3

Some paragraph numbers for and language in the Book of Discipline *may have changed in the 2012 revision, which was published after these Guidelines were printed. We regret any inconvenience.*

MANUFACTURED IN THE UNITED STATES OF AMERICA

Contents

Called to a Ministry of Faithfulness and Vitality

You are so important to the life of the Christian church! You have consented to join with other people of faith who, through the millennia, have sustained the church by extending God's love to others. You have been called and have committed your unique passions, gifts, and abilities to a position of leadership. This Guideline will help you understand the basic elements of that ministry within your own church and within The United Methodist Church.

Leadership in Vital Ministry

Each person is called to ministry by virtue of his or her baptism, and that ministry takes place in all aspects of daily life, both in and outside of the church. Your leadership role requires that you will be a faithful participant in the **mission of the church,** which is to partner with God to **make disciples of Jesus Christ for the transformation of the world.** You will not only engage in your area of ministry, but will work to empower others to be in ministry as well. The vitality of your church, and the church as a whole, depends upon the faith, abilities, and actions of all who work together for the glory of God.

Clearly then, as a pastoral leader or leader among the laity, your ministry is not just a "job," but a spiritual endeavor. You are a spiritual leader now, and others will look to you for spiritual leadership. What does this mean?

All persons who follow Jesus are called to grow spiritually through the practice of various Christian habits (or "means of grace") such as prayer, Bible study, private and corporate worship, acts of service, Christian conferencing, and so on. Jesus taught his disciples practices of spiritual growth and leadership that you will model as you guide others. As members of the congregation grow through the means of grace, they will assume their own role in ministry and help others in the same way. This is the cycle of disciple making.

The Church's Vision

While there is one mission—to make disciples of Jesus Christ—the portrait of a successful mission will differ from one congregation to the next. One of your roles is to listen deeply for the guidance and call of God in your own context. In your church, neighborhood, or greater community, what are the greatest needs? How is God calling your congregation to be in a ministry of service and witness where they are? What does vital ministry look like in the life of your congregation and its neighbors? What are the characteristics, traits, and actions that identify a person as a faithful disciple in your context? This portrait, or vision, is formed when you and the other leaders discern together how your gifts from God come together to fulfill the will of God.

Assessing Your Efforts

We are generally good at deciding what to do, but we sometimes skip the more important first question of what we want to accomplish. Knowing where you are headed (the mission) and knowing what results you want (the vision of your church) are the first two steps in a vital ministry. The third step is in knowing how you will assess or measure the results of what you do and who you are (and become) because of what you do. Those measures relate directly to mission and vision, and they are more than just numbers.

One of your leadership tasks will be to take a hard look, with your team, at all the things your ministry area does or plans to do. No doubt they are good and worthy activities; the question is, "Do these activities and experiences lead people into a mature relationship with God and a life of deeper discipleship?" That is the business of the church, and the church needs to do what only the church can do. You may need to eliminate or alter some of what you do if it does not measure up to the standard of faithful disciple making. It will be up to your ministry team to establish the specific standards against which you compare all that you do and hope to do. (This Guideline includes further help in establishing goals, strategies, and measures for this area of ministry.)

The Mission of The United Methodist Church

Each local church is unique, yet it is a part of a *connection*, a living organism of the body of Christ. Being a connectional church means in part that every local United Methodist church is interrelated through the structure and organization of districts, conferences, and jurisdictions in the larger "family" of the denomination. *The Book of Discipline of The United Methodist Church* describes, among other things, the ministry of all United Methodist Christians, the essence of servant ministry and leadership, how to organize and accomplish that ministry, and how our connectional structure works (see especially ¶¶126–138).

Our Church extends way beyond your doorstep; it is a global Church with both local and international presence. You are not alone. The resources of the entire denomination are intended to assist you in ministry. With this help and the partnership of God and one another, the mission continues. You are an integral part of God's church and God's plan!

(For help in addition to this Guideline and the *Book of Discipline*, see "Resources" at the end of your Guideline, www.umc.org, and the other websites listed on the inside back cover.)

Using This Guideline

t his Guideline is designed to help you, the local church historian, in your ministry. This manual also serves as a companion to the DVD, *Memory and Ministry: Caring for Your Church's Heritage,* which offers specific training in the collection, arrangement, preservation, and interpretation of local church records. The DVD is available from Ecufilm, 810 Twelfth Avenue, South, Nashville, TN 37203; or call 1-800-251-4091.

This Is Your Job

y our basic responsibilities as local church historian are described in ¶247.5a of the *Book of Discipline.* Work with your pastor(s) and church staff, the Committee on Records and History (if one exists), and lay leadership to design procedures that will help you fulfill your duties as described in the *Book of Discipline.*

As historian, you will want to accept the following responsibilities:
- Establish an archives if one does not already exist
- Encourage church officers to keep accurate church records
- Provide for the preservation of all records and historical materials no longer in current use
- Promote interest in the history and heritage of The United Methodist Church and of your own congregation
- Assist the pastor and others in the annual observance of Heritage Sunday and in the celebration of significant anniversaries
- Serve as a member of the Committee on Records and History, if one exists in your congregation
- Serve on the church council and/or other committees to which the local church historian is assigned
- Help those who wish to do research in your church's records

These are the basics. Don't be afraid to branch out, though! Work with your pastor and other church leaders to identify the places and times where you can use your God-given abilities and interests to serve the church in the ministry of history. You may have special gifts in writing, drama, music, working with children, or public relations. Use them to make history come alive! Design a job description and set goals that not only include your basic responsibilities but also suit you and your abilities. Circulate it to the church leadership so that everyone knows that the church historian is an active, vital part of the church's ministry.

The historian's job is a demanding one if it is done well. If the church does not already have a Committee on Records and History, it might be wise to establish one so that others can share the responsibilities.

Other persons and organizations are ready to help you. Among them are your annual conference Commission on Archives and History, the General Commission on Archives and History, state and local libraries and historical societies, and other local church historians in your area. Don't hesitate to ask for their assistance. If they cannot help you, they will be able to recommend someone who can. (See Resources for more information.)

The Ministry of Memory

Why Does History Matter?

History's importance is that it helps us understand who we are. It is a clue to our own identity. Your church's present-day location, its architecture, its worship style, its organization, its ministries and outreach, and countless other facets of its life are all rooted in the history of the congregation. By reflecting on the past, we can better understand who we are and can determine the future directions of our ministry. Memory shapes our vision for ministry.

History can also be a source of *inspiration*. As we learn more about those who created the heritage of which we are heirs, we may be inspired to give thanks for their lives, and we may pledge to follow their example. On the other hand, we recognize that history is made by people who are not always at their best, and their stories can challenge us to learn from their mistakes.

History can provide much enjoyment and can contribute to the pleasure of learning. It is fascinating to learn about the people of the past. We enjoy listening, seeing, and reading about what has happened in the past. Many in your congregation will be captivated by the stories of people and events in your church's history.

History is ministry! Your job is an important part of the church's ministry as you help it record and remember its service for Christ. You participate in the "ministry of memory."

What Are Archives?

have you ever noticed how often we use the same word in a variety of ways? *Archives* can refer to a storage place for historically important records. But *archives* can also refer to the records themselves. In this section we describe just what we mean by historical records and other terms used in this Guideline.

- *Accession:* When records are added to an archives, the transaction is called an accession.
- *Accession list or register:* A simple form listing each accession, the date it was received, and the name of the person(s) or office who gave the materials.
- *Acid-free paper:* Paper having a pH of 7.0 or greater. It is now commonly available in many office supplies stores.
- *Acquisition policy:* Every archival depository must decide which materials it will and will not add to its collection. An acquisition policy briefly summarizes that information.
- *Administrative value:* Records have administrative or operational value when they are needed by an office, an organization, or a person in order to conduct business now and in the future.
- *Archives:* (1) The documents created or received and accumulated by a person or organization in the course of the conduct of affairs and preserved because of their continuing value. (2) The building or part of a building where archival materials are located; can also be called an archival repository.
- *Archives box or container:* A container that stores and protects various types of archival materials.
- *Arrangement:* The process of sorting, organizing, and shelving records so that they can be readily retrieved and used.
- *Collection:* (1) The total group of records created by a person, an institution, or an organization. (2) The total holdings of an archival repository.
- *Correspondence:* Any form of addressed and written communication sent and received, including letters, postcards, memoranda, and notes.
- *Current records:* Records that should stay in office files because they are needed to conduct current business.
- *Deed of gift:* A contract establishing conditions governing the transfer of title to documents and specifying any restrictions on access or use. They are signed by the donor and by a person representing the repository.
- *Description:* The process of describing archival holdings so that researchers can easily understand their contents.

- *Document:* Information recorded in any format, from paper to computer file.
- *Donor:* A person, group, or institution that gives materials to an archival repository.
- *Encapsulation:* Placing a paper document in a clear plastic envelope (usually polyester) and sealing the edges with special tape. This supports and protects fragile items, but still allows them to be viewed and handled.
- *Evidential value:* Records have evidential value when they provide evidence of a person's, organization's, or institution's origins, functions, and activities.
- *File:* A group of documents collected in a folder or a volume.
- *Files:* All or part of the records of an office or agency.
- *Finding aid:* A document that specifically describes all or part of an archives' holdings. It is usually designed to be used by interested persons to locate information in the archives.
- *Guide:* A document that describes all or part of an archives' holdings. It is not as specific as a finding aid.
- *Holdings:* All of the materials held by an archival repository.
- *Inactive records:* See noncurrent records.
- *Informational value:* Documents have informational value when they contain helpful and interesting data. This is distinct from any evidential value they may have.
- *Manuscript:* A handwritten or typed document.
- *Minutes:* Memoranda or notes of a proceeding.
- *Noncurrent records:* Records no longer needed to conduct current business.
- *Personal papers:* The documents belonging to an individual.
- *Processing:* The activities of caring for records: adding them to the archives (accession), organizing them (arrangement and description), preparing finding aids, and properly storing them.
- *Record:* A document created by or for a person, organization, or institution.
- *Records center:* A place where semicurrent records are stored until decisions are made about their ultimate disposition.
- *Records center carton/container:* A specially designed corrugated cardboard box.
- *Repository:* A place where archives are housed; also called a depository.
- *Semicurrent records:* Records that are needed occasionally by an office or a person.
- *Stacks:* The shelved storage area in a library or archives repository.

Putting the Pieces Together

Step 1: Survey the Church's Records

The history of your church is like a big jigsaw puzzle. The puzzle pieces are the documents and other materials that have recorded your church's story since its founding. The following steps will help you put the pieces together.

1. How do you create a good church archives? First, discover what you already have. If your church does not have an archives or historical room, start with a survey. You must journey through your church to discover where its records are kept.

2. Before you begin the actual survey, create a list of the various groups in your church. Such a list can be found in your charge conference reports. (You may know of another place where such a list exists.) Identify the groups that create the records in your church, such as the charge conference or the church council and its various committees.

   Records are also created by Sunday school classes, youth groups, United Methodist Women and United Methodist Men, and other fellowship groups. Special occasions leave records (daily vacation Bible school, a missions outreach project, or a centennial celebration). Be as comprehensive as you can. If your church is the result of a merger, remember to include any groups that were in your predecessor congregations.

3. Now you are ready to survey the church's records. Some records, of course, will be in the office of the church secretary, the church administrator, or the financial officer, not to mention the pastor's office. Records may be in desks, closets, or bookcases; under staircases and behind doors; in the attic or the boiler room; in Sunday school classrooms or the custodian's office.

4. Let people know what you are doing before you begin. Work with the pastor and church staff to examine the records on hand in the church office. With the staff's cooperation, explore other offices and rooms of the church.

5. Make a list of the records you find, noting their dates, condition, and location. This list does not have to be fancy. It is a tool to help you discover what you have in your church and where it is located. A little later we will talk about bringing the material together and arranging it.

LOCATING MISSING RECORDS

After you complete the list, organize the information so that you can determine what records may be missing.

You may find, for instance, that you have financial ledgers for every decade but the 1940s, that you could locate only one Women's Society minute book, and that membership records are complete from the date the church was founded to the present time.

Your next task is to discover what records may be in the hands of church members. This can be a delicate assignment, for persons often feel a real sense of ownership of church records and believe that they will take better care of them than the church historian. You will be most successful when you (with the pastor's help) can communicate a feeling of shared responsibility and stewardship to the congregation. It is important to stress that the church's records tell the story of the whole church family and belong where everyone can have access to them.

One way to approach the task is to make a list of records that you know are missing. Circulate the list among the congregation, former officials, pastors who have moved away, and children of deceased members. Invite their cooperation in collecting missing records.

Be sure to contact your annual conference Commission on Archives and History to determine whether any church records have been deposited at your conference archives. If you are unsure about whom to contact, check the most recent conference journal in the church office or the contact directories at www.gcah.org. The conference archives contain other sources of information about your church, including conference journals and newspapers.

Records may have also found their way to a local public library or historical society. In addition, it will be helpful for you to survey local and regional newspapers from the years since your church's founding. There you will find descriptions of the church's programs; articles about members; birth, wedding, and funeral reports; and feature stories about special church events. Photocopies of this valuable information will enrich your church's archives.

Occasionally, someone will want to donate personal belongings to the archives. If you wish to accept such a gift, you will find it helpful to have a donor agreement form (approved by the charge conference). Having this form avoids future confusion over the ownership of the items. Your local historical society or library may have a donor form that you can use as a model, or you can use the language suggested below:

> I, *(donor name)*, own the items described below. I do hereby give and deliver the property described below to the *(name of church)*. I understand that, unless excepted below, I am giving *(name of church)* full ownership of this property, including copyright without limitation in the right to reproduce, adapt, publish, perform, or publicly display the property. Any part of the property that is not retained by *(name of church)* should be *(select one of the following)* returned to me, disposed of by the church, other *(explain)*.

The agreement should be signed and dated by the church historian and the donor. Keep a copy of the agreement, and provide a copy for the donor along with an expression of appreciation.

Step 2: Understand What to Keep and What to Throw Away

One of the biggest challenges of caring for church records is knowing what should be kept and what should be discarded. Many questions will arise as you survey the materials in the church, as persons give you items for the archives and as you begin to collect minutes, reports, and other materials from church committees and organizations. The first question is, What should I keep? The answer can be complicated, for there is not a hard-and-fast rule that applies to all churches.

Some of your decisions about what to keep will be based on factors you cannot control. The size of your church, both in membership and in its physical plant, will affect your ability to retain the records of your past. If your storage area is very small, you will be able to save only the most vital records. If your church has saved very few records from the past, virtually everything you can find is a valuable record. On the other hand, if you are fortunate enough to have an abundance of records, you can afford to be a little more selective about what you will keep.

Some records should be kept for a few years but then may be discarded. These records help the church do its business efficiently and usually include financial records like canceled checks, invoices, and records of giving.

Certain financial records may need to be kept permanently, depending on the laws in your town, city, or state. In most cases the majority of your financial records do not need to be kept for historical reasons. But be sure to check with your church legal counsel or financial officer before throwing those records away. If you determine that such records do not have historical value, notify the appropriate person(s) so that the records can be destroyed when they are no longer needed.

Other materials may be kept if you find them of historical interest and have room for them, but these are not vital documents and may be discarded. In this category are office calendars, office memos, budget worksheets, and general correspondence. These can be thrown away when they no longer serve any useful purpose in your church office. Once a year, for example, the church secretary can dispose of general correspondence that is at least one year old. (However, you may want to keep correspondence that documents some special function of your church, such as a particular service to the community.)

In doing your survey, you may have discovered that you have multiple copies of some items. People may also give you copies of material you already have. You can ask that the church approve the policy that no more than two of the same item be kept. Doing that will ensure wise and efficient use of your space, which is always limited.

Finally, before you throw materials away, consider whether they may be of interest to another archives or library. For example, it is not necessary to save local newspapers in your church archives, but your town or county historical society may be very interested in adding them to its collection.

Copies or originals of important records should be stored offsite, perhaps in a local bank or other secure place. Some of these records may well exist in electronic format (such as membership databases). Copies of these electronic records should be stored offsite and frequently updated by replacing the older files with the most recent copies. For more information, consult the GCAH website (www.gcah.org) and look for the manual titled, *Guidelines for Managing Records of the Local Church and Annual Conference and Guidelines for Managing Electronic Records*.

KEEP THESE RECORDS!
Description

Administrative reports	Permanent
Charge conference reports, administrative board or church council reports	Permanent
Architectural drawings, blueprints, maps, legal documents, and deeds	Permanent

Annual budget	Permanent
Sunday worship bulletins and bulletins printed for special occasions	Permanent
Local church committee records	Permanent
Directories	Permanent
Membership registers, baptisms, marriages, and transfers	Permanent
Church newsletters, UMW, UMM, UMYF, and other church group newsletters	Permanent
Scrapbooks, photographs, mementos of special occasions	Permanent

ELECTRONIC RECORDS ISSUES

The management of electronic records usually revolves around word processing documents. To gain an idea of the complexity of the problem one only needs to consider the different number of word processing formats in use. Just from the recent past there are over 48 different word processing file formats. If an archives wanted to maintain the electronic files in their native format it would need more than 40 different word processing programs to deal with all of these formats. It would need not only the programs but also the operating system on which the program was designed to run.

In the past twenty years there have been at least six different operating systems and a variety of versions under those six. It quickly becomes obvious why an archives cannot maintain electronic files in their native format. Electronic files, in order to be used, are dependent on software and hardware. This dependency makes them extremely vulnerable over time to loss due to changes in technology and the market. And this doesn't even touch the issue of the stability of the medium on which electronic records are stored.

To preserve an electronic file for the future, it either needs to be converted to some standardized electronic format or printed. While there are standardized formats for both electronic document files and for databases that are supported by the archival and technological communities, they are minimalist file formats, which means that much of the formatting of a document will be lost and some of the flexibility of complex databases will also be lost. The most secure way to deal with most electronic documents is to print out the document on paper. The document can then easily be managed under records retention guidelines.

But not every type of electronic record can be printed so in managing such files there are several points that must be kept in mind.

• The first is migrating the records when operating systems or software are upgraded. This is one of the most easily overlooked issues. Most offices have a variety of records on their hard drives, servers, and back-up media like CDs. When a computer's operating system or software is upgraded, the data files need to be migrated as well. This usually isn't a problem for the files stored on the computer or server, which are probably used on a regular basis. But files on older backup media like USB drives, and CDs may be overlooked and might be no longer accessible when they are finally used. This could especially be the case if the files were created more than two upgrades ago. When software or operating systems are upgraded, you want to make sure that all of your files can be accessed by the new system. Take the time to open and access files especially on your backup media and if necessary open them all and save them in the new format. And don't assume that the upgrade of the same product will mean that your files are always accessible. If you are going to keep records in an electronic format, always make sure that you migrate them along with each operating system or product upgrade.

• Organizing your computer's file system is another important element. The same retention guidelines apply to electronic files as to paper files. Many users just store files on their hard drives without any planning. Some use minimal planning. This has negative consequences in several areas. The first is a degradation of your computer's performance. Folders (or directories) that contain a large number of files are inefficient for the computer. It takes more memory and time to manage a large number of files in a single folder. It is also takes longer to search a large folder or directory, either visually or with a search engine. As much as possible, replicate your paper filing structure on your computer. This will make it easier for the computer to manage itself and for you to manage your files. Where appropriate, make sure you can distinguish between files that do not need to be kept from those that have a longer or permanent retention. You can do this either by creating appropriate folders or by a naming convention. This makes backup easier, and it makes management of your files easier. Copying entire directories is much faster than hunting through a long file list.

• Making backups is probably the most important task to be done. Computers do wear out and cease to operate, causing all information on them to be lost. Offices are damaged during storms and vandalism happens. Where are you keeping copies of your data? Backing up data is the most difficult thing to do, as it takes time and seems unproductive. But without it, after an accident, productivity will really cease. In a networked environment it is a little easier to back up data. Files can be stored on the server and the server automated to make backups on a regular basis. But in the small office the single-user computer also needs to be backed up. That may be as simple as copying files to a USB drive on a daily basis, or using a backup program. And for very important files you will want to store the copies somewhere else than at work, just as you do for important papers. This has been touched on in the "Vital Records section of *Guidelines for Managing Records of the Local Church and Annual Conference* which can be found at http://www.gcah.org.

It is worth mentioning, as a final note, the longevity of some electronic media. None of the electronic storage media has as long a shelf life as does acid-free paper. USB drives and hard drives all have about a 25-year life expectancy. There have been several claims about the longevity of CDs. There are also questions about stability regarding the technology that allows the CDs to be read. Just as there are hardly any computers now that can read 8-inch floppy disks, diskettes, or Zip drives, the next generation of CD readers won't be able to read earlier CD versions. This is another way of emphasizing the importance of migration. Not only must electronic records be migrated as operating and software systems change, but they must be migrated as storage systems change as well. It doesn't matter how long the media lasts if there is no equipment left that can read the media.

For more information see our Electronic Records Guidelines at www.gcah.org.

Step 3: Organize Your Records
The next step in creating your archives is organizing and arranging the records that you located in your survey (Step 1) and decided to keep (Step 2). This third step is important so that you and others can have easy access to the church's records (and therefore its memory).

The two lists you created in Step 1 will come in handy now. They are, first, the list of the groups and organizations in your local church and, second, the list noting what records you located and where they currently may be found in the church. Now is the time to physically bring those records together in one place and to arrange them.

This presupposes that you will have some place to put the records once you have arranged them. (See "Step 4: Caring for Your Records" for information about the appropriate kind of space to store records.) "Like goes with like" is the best rule for arranging your records. Using the list of groups in your church as a guide, sort the materials by their connection to those groups.

1. Assemble all the records of a particular group. For example, if you found administrative board minutes in the basement, attic, and the pastor's closet, put all of those records together. Do the same for all the other groups.

2. Sort each group by record type. For example, the church council group may include minutes, reports, and long-range plans. Place all the minutes together in chronological order. Do the same for reports and then the long-range plans. A Sunday school group might have a class newsletter and photographs from various events. Sort the newsletters by date and then the photographs.

3. Sort some records, like correspondence files, alphabetically. Even though you can often sort records by their dates, it is not always the correct way to arrange materials.

4. On each file folder write (in pencil) the name of the group (such as "Administrative Board" or "Church Council") and the type of record (such as "minutes") and the dates covered by the material in the file folder. Note the same information on a separate list.

5. If your local church is the result of a merger of other churches and if you have their records, as you should, keep those records separate. In a case like this, the arrangement is a little more complicated. For example, we can imagine the case of two churches, St. Luke's and St. John's, which merged into a third, St. Paul's. Your arrangement should reflect each predecessor church. So you would create a list titled "St. Luke's" in which you would identify all the records related to that church. You would repeat the process for St. John's and for St. Paul's.

6. Consider one final note on arrangement. If your church is old enough, and it probably is, you will notice that some organizations have gone through several name changes. For example, the Woman's Society of Christian Service and the Wesleyan Service Guild were names of groups that later became United Methodist Women; the Fourth Quarterly Conference became the charge conference, and the board of stewards was followed by the board of trustees. What should be done about these name changes and reorganizations? The easiest method is to arrange all the groups alphabetically, no matter when they existed.

This is the simplest approach by far and the recommended one in most cases. But it does require you to remember the connections between groups as they change names and split apart.

7. The other possibility is to arrange the material by functions within the local church. Within the function group you can arrange the material chronologically. The following function groups are suggested: Administrative, Sunday Schools, Women, Men, and Youth. Underneath each function you can then place the groups that dealt with similar concerns.

This approach can be useful if you have many records from each predecessor group or if you have very few records from the predecessor groups and don't want them to get lost while you are organizing. Your church (or a church that merged with yours) may have belonged to one of the denominations that predates The United Methodist Church. The following information will help you sort out the records that belong to each denomination:

The United Methodist Church and Its Predecessors

Methodist Episcopal Church (1784–1939)
Methodist Episcopal Church, South (1844–1939)
Methodist Protestant Church (1830–1939)
The Methodist Church (1939–1968)
Church of the United Brethren in Christ (1800–1946)
Evangelical Association (1803–1922)
United Evangelical Church (1894–1922)
Evangelical Church (1922–1946)
Evangelical United Brethren Church (1946–1968)
The United Methodist Church (1968–present)

Step 4: Care for Your Records
Here are some ways to prolong the life of your church's records:
1. Unfold all documents to their full size for permanent storage. Folded papers will eventually tear at the fold. You may need to provide a special storage area for oversized material.
2. Remove rubber bands, which deteriorate over time and adhere to documents. Also remove paper clips, staples, and other fasteners. Metal fasteners can rust. They also catch and cause tears as you remove documents from folders.
3. Place your records in acid-free file folders and store them in acid-free containers, which are specially designed to help protect your documents. See page 35 for a list of suppliers.

4. Make photocopies on acid-free paper of newspaper clippings you wish to save. This can be done for any item that has important information printed on poor quality paper. See page 35 for a list of suppliers.

5. Place fragile documents in Mylar or polyethylene covers, which will provide additional support to the paper when handling is necessary. See page 35 for a list of suppliers.

6. Learn how to encapsulate documents. This will give greater protection to some of your older records. Don't confuse this with lamination, which should be avoided. Regional and local historical societies or libraries should be able to assist you.

7. Store photographs and negatives in isolation from other materials. They can be stored singly in acid-free, Mylar, or polyethylene envelopes, or collectively in a folder as long as a piece of acid-free paper is placed between each image. It is best to write all identifying information either on the envelope or in the front or back margin of the photograph. Pens especially designed for this purpose are available. See page 35 for a list of suppliers.

8. Do not write on or mark the papers in your custody. Be sure that persons using the archives do not underline or mark the documents in any way.

9. If papers become water-soaked, move them to a dry storage area. Place an electric fan in the area and dry at normal temperatures. The fan is necessary to create moving air. Mold is more likely to grow if the air is still.

10. If there is evidence of bugs or vermin in your archives, have the area fumigated. Check over your records carefully to see if there is any infestation in the boxes. If so, isolate the boxes with appropriate bug traps.

11. Use only archival mending tape when making minor repairs.

12. Use a permanent black ink pen to take handwritten minutes and other local church records.

13. Use acid-free paper for all of your permanent records, such as reports and minutes.

14. Create scrapbooks with acid-free materials only.

15. Attach scrapbook items in such a way that the items can be removed without damage either to themselves or the scrapbook pages. Use corner holders, water-soluble glue, or Mylar sheets. Avoid cellophane and transparent tapes, which will discolor with age, shrink, become brittle, and eventually detach, leaving ugly and damaging yellow stains on the material.

16. Treat the contents of cornerstone boxes with special care. Careless or improper handling of the box itself may even damage the items

inside. Arrange to copy the contents immediately after opening the box. Avoid using cornerstones in the future. They do not protect the items well. If your church wants to preserve something for future members to look at, invest the time and funds into a church archives/history room.

17. Always feel free to ask for help or advice. Contact local historical societies, your annual conference Commission on Archives and History, or the General Commission on Archives and History if you have questions.

18. Having taken the time to protect your records by placing them in the proper containers, think about the type of room in which to store them.

19. The storage room should be cool and dry. If nothing else, a relatively constant temperature and humidity will help preserve your records. Avoid placing your archives in either the attic or the basement. A temperature between 65 degrees and 70 degrees Fahrenheit with around 48 percent relative humidity is ideal.

20. Storing the items and boxes on steel shelving is better than on wood. Most wood has been treated in a manner similar to standard boxes and file folders. Given time the wood will damage your storage containers.

21. Your items will be more secure if the storage area can be locked and only a limited number of people have access to the keys.

22. Your records should be kept in a fireproof or fire-resistant room or storage area if possible. Your storage area should have smoke alarms wired into your general alarm system for the entire church.

23. You are wise to keep a fire extinguisher handy, preferably two: one for paper fires and another for electrical fires.

Step 5: Manage the Records

If we are to have a past for the future, we must preserve the records of today. This is the function of records management.

A records management program strives to achieve economy and efficiency in the creation, use, maintenance, and disposal of church records.

Effective use of space and time. After personnel costs, keeping records is one of the largest administrative expenditures in the church. Record creation, maintenance, filing, office storage space, filing supplies, and equipment all contribute to the high cost of keeping records.

Legal protection. If your church is ever faced with legal action, having a records management program in place can assure courts and litigants that records are being disposed of properly and in a routine manner, not maliciously or capriciously.

Records management is the attempt to systematically control the growth and disposition, or destruction, of your records. Its basic purpose is to help answer those nagging questions: What do I keep? How long do I keep it? and When can I remove it from my office?

Now we need to define some terms. In every office, a variety of records are related because they result from the same filing process, or the same function, or the same activity, or have a similar form or content. This group of related documents is called a series. For example, file folders of bank statements from different banks are a series, as are a collection of invoices or of staff memos. For each series there are two important questions to be asked. The first is, *How are these records used?*—this is referred to as the *records life cycle*. The second is, *How significant are these records?*—this is referred to as *appraisal*.

RECORDS LIFE CYCLE

Records are almost living organisms. They are born, mature during their use, and then are retired or removed. In records management, the task is to recognize when a record has reached the end of its life cycle or no longer serves a useful administrative function. In general, the less a record is consulted, the less useful it is administratively. When a record has reached the end of its useful administrative function, it is ready to be retired from the office. The function of appraisal helps us determine when to retire the record and what to do with the record once it is retired.

RECORDS APPRAISAL

Appraisal is the process by which we determine the administrative, legal, and fiscal value (primary value) and the historical and long-term research value (secondary value) of records. Once the value of a record series has been determined, a realistic retention period can be assigned to it. Appraisal can take place at any point during a record series' life cycle, but it is most frequently done when the records become inactive.

There are several questions to be asked when appraising a series: How frequently is the record used by those who created it? If the record is still frequently consulted, then it should probably remain in the office. If the record is not consulted frequently, is there still a consistent, although low, demand for it? Is there some legal or fiscal need to hold on to the record even though it is no longer consulted or used? An example is financial information.

What is the historical significance of the record? By and large, records with historical significance provide information about the church, such as charge conference records or church council ministries.

Records management is something that can be handled at the local church level. You can do it with the help of your church's legal counsel, your annual conference Commission on Archives and History, and the General Commission on Archives and History. The General Commission on Archives and History (GCAH) has published a set of guidelines that can help your local church establish its own retention schedules. You may purchase *Guidelines for Managing Records of the Local Church and the Annual Conference* by contacting GCAH or you may download the document for free from the GCAH website at www.gcah.org. A reasonable program can be set up so that what needs to be saved for the archives will be saved and what needs to be protected for the successful administration of your church's ministry will be preserved.

Step 6: Tell Your Church's Story to the Future

We create history every day of our lives, as individuals and as church congregations. Yesterday's worship service or committee meeting is today's history. Part of your responsibility as church historian is to document the unfolding story of your church.

One way to approach the task of saving today's history is to ask yourself what you would like to know about your church's past. Are those kinds of stories and records from today being preserved now for tomorrow? Imagine your church a century from now trying to discover what the congregation was like in the 1990s and early 2000s. How did we worship? What social issues most concerned us? What were our mission and evangelism outreaches? What was Sunday school like? What music did we sing? Who were the people active in our church's life and ministry? How did we have fun?

You know that your church's history is more than the names of its pastors and the dates when new buildings were constructed. The story of the church is the story of the whole congregation: pastors, Sunday school teachers, choirs, youth groups, mission circles, men, women, and children. Your challenge is to collect those records and artifacts that will help tell an inclusive, three-dimensional story of today's church for tomorrow's researcher.

Your own enthusiasm for the task of locating local church history sources will spark enthusiasm in others. Your most valuable resource may be a network of persons who care as you do about recovering local church history.

- Ask persons to give you newspaper clippings with references to church members. Photocopy them and keep them in a human-interest file.
- Videotape a typical Sunday morning worship service.
- Enlist an enthusiastic photographer to shoot a week in the life of the church, covering everything from worship to committee meetings, choir practice to Mom's Day Out. Make sure that all photos are identified!
- Ask Sunday school classes of children, youth, and adults to respond in writing to the question, "I like our church because..." in order to capture a sense of the congregation's personality.
- Invite the youth group to create a video tour of the church and its programs. Not only will you document the daily life of the church but you'll also get a good idea of what today's young people think is important.
- Do an oral history project (see below).

Whether your church is new or old, struggling or thriving, the story of its people and its ministry should be preserved for future generations. The record of what God has wrought through your local church is worthy of being saved. God is alive and working in congregations, young and old, large and small, rural and urban. The story must be recorded and shared. Let us be responsible for sharing the tradition with future generations.

DOING ORAL HISTORY

As you read through your church's records, do you wish you could ask *What was it really like?* Dry statistics and bland reports suddenly come to life when we hear the personal stories of the people involved. Those stories from long ago are lost to us; but with an oral history project, it is possible to preserve today's stories for the future.

In the past, we could only rely on the written word for our records. Today, with audio-video recording, we can record people's memories in their own voices, with the shading, nuance, and emphasis that give language its emotion and richness. Oral history interviews record eyewitness accounts of important events, significant persons, trends, changes, and continuity in the life of your church. The memories of church members add detail and dimension to the basic facts recorded in documents.

BEFORE YOU BEGIN

An oral history project takes time, careful planning, and commitment. Before you begin, ask yourself what you want the project to accomplish. Will you focus on gathering the stories of your older members? Will the emphasis be on a particular era (such as World War II) or on a crucial event in the life of the church (such as its involvement in a particular mission)? Do you want this to be an intergenerational experience, comparing perceptions and experiences of different age groups?

As you define the project, draw up a list of persons (narrators) you would like to interview. The church staff and other congregational leaders may also be able to offer suggestions. Invite each narrator well ahead of time and describe the project carefully. You may even want to write out a page of information, or even some questions, for your narrators so that they know what is expected of them. It is a good policy to prepare a statement for both the interviewer and the narrator to sign that will permit others to use the information gathered in the interview. This will help the narrator understand that the interview will become part of the church's records.

Develop a realistic schedule for the interviews. You will be exhausted if you try to do twenty-five interviews in a two-week period! Pace yourself so that your own enthusiasm and interest remain high. Each interview should feel fresh, even if you have asked some of the questions a dozen times before.

Make sure you are comfortable with your equipment before you begin. The narrator will relax and speak more naturally if the tape recorder or video camera is unobtrusive.

WHAT DO YOU WANT TO KNOW?
Remember that the interview should not simply record information available elsewhere. Rather, it should supplement and clarify written records. The direction of the interview will depend in part upon your goals for the oral history project and in part on the personality and experience of the narrator. One or two casual conversations with the narrator in the days and weeks leading up to the interview will help you determine what subject areas you can cover.

Come to the interview with a list of subject areas and tentative questions. These will help you direct the interview. The subject areas you cover will reflect the narrator's personal history as well as the oral history project's focus, but general areas will be of interest in all but the most tightly focused interviews. These include the following:

- the narrator's family background
- how he or she first became involved with your church
- earliest memories of church participation

- descriptions of worship experiences
- memories of major events in the life of the church
- reminiscences of people
- descriptions of the community in different eras
- opinions on matters that have had a major impact on the church
- the narrator's feelings and thoughts about the church today.

CONDUCTING THE INTERVIEW

Your task as the interviewer is to encourage the narrator to tell his or her story. You should guide the narrator with brief questions, but this is not the place for you to share your own memories.

Start the interview with background questions, such as where the narrator was born, when he or she joined the church, and basic family information. This will help both you and the narrator become comfortable with the interview process.

After establishing basic facts, it is time to move into the body of the interview. Use the list of subject areas and tentative questions that you prepared earlier. You will need to be both firm and flexible. It is important not to let the interview stray too far into subjects that are not really relevant, but it is important to allow the narrator to talk about those things that are important to him or her. Don't interrupt a good story because you think you must adhere to your outline. However, be sure to ask the questions that you think need to be addressed in the interview.

What kinds of questions should you ask? Use the reporter's "who, what, when, where, how, and why" method. The question, "Was Rev. Smith a good preacher?" may get a one-word response, but the question, "What was Rev. Smith's preaching style?" will give the narrator a chance to describe, interpret, and reminisce.

The narrator may not always have the facts straight. All of us get a little confused about dates and other details. Avoid confronting the narrator if you know that what you are hearing is incorrect, unless it is absolutely critical to the story. It is the essence of the story that counts—the narrator's thoughts, feelings, reactions, impressions, interpretations, and analysis. Editorial corrections can be made in the typed transcript if necessary (for example, "The church burned down in 1971." [1972, ed.]).

Be careful not to bombard the narrator with too many questions all at once or with lengthy, rambling questions. Be brief and to the point! Remember that you are not the star of the interview. As long as your questions draw out the narrator, they do not have to be brilliantly phrased or eloquently delivered.

Relax! Don't worry about filling every moment with dialogue. Let the narrator pause to think about a response or to remember a detail. Your instinct may be to jump in with a question every time there are a few seconds of silence, but wait until you are sure the narrator is ready to move on.

Be sensitive to the narrator. If you sense that he or she is tiring, take a break. Ninety minutes is probably the maximum amount of time for an interview. If you feel there is more to talk about, arrange to meet another time. Choose a comfortable setting for the interview. Make sure that you have a pitcher of water and some tissues handy. Some people will be glad to come to the church or to your home, while others will be able to relax only in their own homes.

There may be times when the comfort level is so high that the narrator may say more than he or she intended. If the discussion becomes very personal and intimate, make sure the narrator remembers that the conversation is being recorded. Try to avoid "off the record" comments as much as possible.

AFTER THE INTERVIEW
Play the recording immediately after the interview, so you can be sure that everything was properly recorded. Write a thank-you note to the narrator, expressing your appreciation for his or her willingness to participate.

In order to preserve the information you have carefully recorded, do two things: copy the recordings to your computer as WAV files, if possible, and create a typed transcript of the interview. Typing a transcript is a time-consuming process and requires accuracy and care. Be sure to have a third person read the transcriptions while listening to the recordings, just to make doubly sure the typed document is accurate.

Writing Your Church's History
Why Write a History?
- To tell the story of God at work in the life of your congregation
- To gather and preserve the record of faithful witnesses through the years
- To teach the members and friends of the congregation, now and in the future

• To help your church see its ministry and mission as an ongoing pilgrimage

Is It Time for a Church History?

When was your last church history written? If it was more than twenty-five years ago, it is probably time for an update. If you have no written history at all, it is certainly time to think seriously about writing one.

Are people in the congregation willing to work on this project? A good history is a collaboration of skilled researchers, writers, and editors. Each person must be enthusiastic, talented, and committed to the project. Even if the history is researched and written by one person, there should still be an editorial committee to support and oversee the project.

Will the church support the project? There must be money to print and promote a church history. Remember, too, that the project needs the approval and support of the pastors and other church leaders.

STARTING THE TASK

The idea for writing a church history may come from the church historian or some other person or group. The church council (or similar body) should approve the project and its financing. It will be helpful if you prepare a detailed plan. Include a rationale for the project (why do we need a church history?), a timeline for production and promotion, and suggestions for funding. Suggest what the final product will look like (how long, what format, and so forth). Looking at histories published by other churches may give you some good ideas.

The project should be assigned to the Committee on Records and History or to a special task force that includes representatives of all the major areas of church life. Your history will only be as good as its author(s). You may want to select one or more persons in the congregation, or you may choose someone who is not a member of the church. If there are multiple authors, designate a chairperson or editor. The writer(s) should be guaranteed their independence in judgment but must be willing to listen to the counsel of a review board whose members will read and criticize the writing as it proceeds. Criticism (both positive and negative) is not easy for some writers to accept, but it is essential to writing a good history.

Develop a project budget that includes all fees and honoraria, mileage and telephone expenses, photocopying and supplies, publication and printing costs, publicity expenses, and the book's purchase price. Perhaps the best way to finance a history is to make the total cost a church budget item (over a three- or four-year period) so that one copy can be distributed to each church family. Sales will seldom cover the entire cost of a history. Funds may be raised by special contributions, or a single donor may provide the funds with the book dedicated to the donor or to someone the donor designates.

CONDUCTING THE RESEARCH

Several people can participate in the research process. Each can be assigned a specific topic (such as women's organizations, pastors' biographies, or architectural changes to the sanctuary). Anyone doing research must be dedicated to digging hard for as many facts as possible. It is up to the writer(s) to interpret those facts.

Sources of information include the church's records, conference journals and newspapers, and local newspapers. Work with the town librarian and the local historical society. Contact your annual conference archives and the General Commission on Archives and History. Examine every available source carefully. Evaluate each source openly and report the information fairly. To do less can result in an inaccurate and incomplete story.

Remember that you are writing for the future as well as the present: identify all persons, places, and events as accurately as possible. Check, recheck, and triple check facts and dates! People will rely on this history for many years to come.

Take care that all persons and groups are properly recognized for their role in the history of the church. The history should not simply document the clergy who have served your congregation.

You may also need to have permission to mention specific people or to use photographs or other materials. If your history is copyrighted, permissions may be necessary.

ORGANIZING THE STORY

The easiest way to organize a historical account is by chronological order: starting with the beginning and coming up to the present. A second method is by periods, such as the early beginnings, a period of great growth, a controversial period, or on the basis of pastors who have served. A third method is by topical arrangement. This basis offers more flexibility but is more difficult to develop than the other two. A typical outline might look like this:

- Profile of the Membership, Past and Present
- Organization of the Congregation
- Buildings and Other Property
- Pastoral and Lay Leadership
- Organization and Activities
- Worship and Music
- Special Occasions
- Service and Mission
- Finances
- Ecumenical and Community Relations

No matter how you choose to organize your history, special touches can enrich the final product. These might include:
- Photographs to enliven the text and provide another window to the past.
- Brief sketches about people and events to add human interest to the story. Consider featuring these vignettes at the beginning of each chapter.
- Information about everyday things paints a picture of the times (the price of postage stamps, fashion trends, favorite radio programs). This helps the reader relate to the lives of historical figures.
- An index and several appendixes (such as financial and membership statistics, lists of pastors, or names of church organizations in different eras). You may want to include a timeline listing various milestones in the church's history.
- Parts that can be placed on your church's website.

WRITING THE STORY

A good church history will faithfully record the past. It can also educate, entertain, and inspire. You want to tell the story of real people's lives, not tabulate dry statistics and lifeless facts. You want to reveal something of the depth, complexity, and texture of church life. Researchers, writers, and editors all need to remember that their goal is to put flesh on the bare bones of history.

It is very important to remember that your church's history has not happened in isolation. It has been a part of the community, both local and national. It has been affected by political events and social change. Its members have been concerned about the events of the world around them. Tell the story of your church in the context of its time and place.

Write clearly and concisely. Use brief, uncomplicated paragraphs. Place frequent subheads in the chapters to enable the reader to follow the account more easily. Don't use too many long quotations, which can interrupt the flow of the narrative. Edit the rough draft carefully to ensure the accuracy of facts and interpretations and to strengthen style. Two or three drafts may be required as the committee provides editorial suggestions to the writer.

PUBLISHING, PROMOTING, AND USING THE HISTORY
Discuss with your printer the appropriate way to prepare the copy, whether it is to be typeset or duplicated from your camera-ready copy.

Promote sales in advance, perhaps with a reduced prepublication price. Consider a special dedication service for releasing the history. Arrange for the writer(s) to be available to autograph copies. Provide a news story to local newspapers and your annual conference.

A church can use its published history in a variety of special ways. Encourage all members to read and study it carefully. Use it in membership orientation and confirmation training. Invite the writer(s) to lead a special study on the church's history and to use the history as the basic text. A question that can be considered in various church groups is, *What does our history tell us about our present responsibility, our future ministry, and our mission as a congregation?*

Be sure to publish enough copies to provide an ample supply for a period of years. Arrange for safe storage and preservation of extra copies, but remember that stored copies over a long period may deteriorate; therefore, reprinting may be cheaper. Present copies to your local library, the annual conference archives, and the General Commission on Archives and History.

MAKING HISTORY COME ALIVE!
One of your most important tasks is to encourage your church to recognize history and heritage as a part of its ministry. Learning about our history helps us learn about ourselves. Seeing how God has been at work in the past helps us see how God is at work in the present. Understanding where we have been helps us make decisions about where we need to go. How does history become a ministry? How can you share with the whole church family the good news of God's work in the church's past? There are as many ways as there are churches. What you decide to do will depend on your resources, your interests, and the help of others.

Observe significant anniversaries, whether your tenth or your hundredth. Plan events that will involve as many people as possible and that will bring history to life for young and old. Two resources provided by the General

Commission on Archives and History can help you. *Celebrating Our United Methodist Heritage: A Resource Packet for the Local Church* is available only online at www.gcah.org and *To Remember and Celebrate: Worship Resources for Heritage Events* is available for sale in hard copy or free online at www.gcah.org. (See pages 33–36 for more information.)

Celebrate Heritage Sunday each year. Heritage Sunday is May 24 or the Sunday preceding that date. May 24 is known as Aldersgate Day, remembering John Wesley's experience of faith on that date in 1738 at a prayer meeting held on Aldersgate Street in London. Heritage Sunday calls the church to remember the past by committing itself to the continuing call of God. The General Commission provides a theme and resources each year.

Many historical projects can be done by the whole church or one of its organizations. Here are several suggestions:

• Prepare a list of the clergy from the United Methodist tradition who are buried in your church or area cemeteries, whether they served your congregation or not. Plan to mark their graves with the official United Methodist minister's grave marker, available from Cokesbury. Secure permission and have the markers installed by a qualified person. Conduct an appropriate service in the cemetery after careful research on the life and times of the pastors. A suggested order of worship is included in *To Remember and Celebrate: Worship Resources for Heritage Events* (see page 33).
• Gather information about all the persons from your church who have entered full-time church vocations. Honor them with a special display and articles in your church newsletter or local newspaper. Add the information you have collected to the church archives so that it will be available to other researchers.
• When you discover bits of historical lore that are unusual—enlightening, dramatic, or funny—find a way to share them with the church family. Perhaps you can initiate a "History Minute" during Sunday morning worship, write a "Did You Know" column in the church newsletter, or speak to Sunday school classes.
• Contact your annual conference Commission on Archives and History or the General Commission on Archives and History to learn what United Methodist historic sites or heritage landmarks are located within a reasonable driving distance. Organize a tour with interested persons from your church.
• Alert your congregation to the historical activities of your annual conference and its Commission on Archives and History. Take other members with you to training events for historians. Get acquainted with the

persons who can provide guidance and support, such as the conference historian or archivist.

• If your conference has a historical society, join it and encourage other members to join also. Enroll in the Historical Society of The United Methodist Church. Join your local historical society so that you can learn how your church's history connects to your community's history.

Resources

GENERAL COMMISSION ON ARCHIVES AND HISTORY
P.O. Box 127, Madison, NJ 07940
(973) 408-3189
FAX (973) 408-3909
www.gcah.org

- *Historical Society Membership.* http://www.historicalsocietyunited methodistchurch.org/membership/ Annual fee includes an optional subscription to *Methodist History* (quarterly journal), *Historian's Digest* (Society newsletter), and additional discounts.
- *Methodist History.* Official historical publication of The United Methodist Church, issued quarterly, containing articles on United Methodist events and personalities, book reviews, and analyses of trends across the years. Write for a brochure. Back issues are available, as is an index for volumes I-XX, 1962–82 and an index for volumes XXI-XXXV, 1982–1997. Available free online at the GCAH website.
- *Archives and History Directory.* Contains names and addresses of history leaders at the annual conference and general church levels. Also contains information about repositories and research centers. Available on GCAH website.
- *Celebrating Our United Methodist Heritage: A Resource for the Local Church.* Contains four sections: the *Planning Guide* identifies times and ways to celebrate and offers tips on organizing events; *A Songbook of Ideas* contains dozens of suggestions for celebrating history; *Voices from Our Past* is a collection of quotations from twenty important figures in United Methodist history, and the *Resource Directory* contains names and addresses that will be helpful to persons planning a heritage celebration. Only available on GCAH website.
- *Telling Their Stories: The History of Women in the Local Church.* Resource packet with tips on oral history projects, exhibit design, and special programs for churches interested in recovering and celebrating the history of women in their own community. The packet also includes a women's history timeline and a suggested reading list. Can be ordered from the GCAH website.
- *To Remember and Celebrate: Worship Resources for Heritage Events.* Contains suggested orders of worship for commemorating a church anniversary, Aldersgate Sunday, Heritage Sunday, installation of a grave marker, consecration of a history room, and other worship experiences. Also includes John Wesley's 1784 Order for Morning Prayer and Order for Administration of the Lord's Supper, Wesley's Orders for Worship, and an Order for a Love Feast. Available free on the GCAH website.

- *Women in the Wesleyan and United Methodist Traditions,* compiled by Susan E. Warrick. A bibliography of more than 800 books, dissertations, and journal articles about the history of women in The United Methodist Church and related denominations. Entries are divided into subject categories, including Missions and Missionaries, Social Reform, Biography, Clergy Wives, Preachers and Evangelists, and John Wesley's Circle. Only available on GCAH website.
- *The Racial and Ethnic Presence in American Methodism: A Bibliography,* compiled by C. Jarrett Gray Jr. Collected titles pertaining to the history of Asian Americans, Hispanics, Native Americans, and African Americans in the United Methodist tradition. Designed to accompany the histories of those groups available from Cokesbury. Can be ordered from GCAH website.
- *Publications.* Write or visit the GCAH website for a current list and order blank for the numerous pamphlets and books on a variety of historical subjects. Titles include pocket-sized booklets on church founders and leaders, bibliographies, manuals, directories, and handbooks.

COKESBURY STORE, (800) 672-1789 OR COKESBURY.COM
- *The Methodist Experience in America: Volume 1,* by Russell E. Richey, Kenneth E. Rowe, and Jean Miller Schmidt (Nashville: Abingdon Press, 2010. ISBN 9780687246724.). And a sourcebook.
- *United Methodism in America: A Compact History,* edited by John G. McEllhenney (Nashville: Abingdon Press, 1992. ISBN 0-687-43170-0).
- *John Wesley: Holiness of Heart and Life* by Charles Yrigoyen, Jr. (Nashville: Abingdon Press, 1999. ISBN 0-687-05686-1).

AMERICAN ASSOCIATION FOR STATE AND LOCAL HISTORY
1717 Church Street, Nashville, TN 37203-2991. (615) 320-3203. www.aaslh.org
This association has the most extensive list of helpful resources of any group in the country. A complete catalog is available from the above address.
- *Oral History for the Local Historical Society,* third edition, revised, by Willa K. Baum.
- *Starting Right: A Basic Guide to Museum Planning,* by Gerald George and Cindy Sherrell-Leo.
- *Historical Celebrations: A Handbook for Organizers of Diamond Jubilees, Centennials, and Other Community Anniversaries,* by Keith Petersen.
- *Local History Collections: A Manual for Librarians,* by Enid T. Thompson.

- *Nearby History: Exploring the Past Around You: Volume 4, Places of Worship,* by James P. Wind.
- *Researching, Writing, and Publishing Local History,* second edition, by Thomas E. Felt.
- *Technical Leaflets* (more than 100 different titles available).

THE SOCIETY OF AMERICAN ARCHIVISTS
17 North State Street
Suite 1425
Chicago, IL 60602-3315
tel 312-606-0722
fax 312-606-0728
toll-free 866-722-7858
www.archivists.org.
- *Keeping Archives,* edited by Judith Ellis.
- *Modern Archives Reader. Basic Readings on Archival Theory and Practice,* edited by Maygene F. Daniels and Timothy Walch.
- *Archival Fundamental Series II series.*

Visit http://www.archivists.org for a complete listing of the publications of the society.

SOURCES FOR ARCHIVAL SUPPLIES
- **Conservation Resources International**
  5532 Port Royal Road, Springfield, VA 22151
  Telephone: (800) 634-6932, (703) 321-7730
  FAX: (703) 321-0629
  http://www.conservationresources.com
- **Gaylord**
  P.O. Box 4901, Syracuse, NY 13221-4901
  Telephone: (800) 962-9580
  FAX: (800) 272-3412
  http://www.gaylord.com
- **The Hollinger Metal Edge**
  California:
  6340 Bandini Blvd., Commerce, CA 90040
  Telephone: (800) 862-2228
  FAX: (888) 822-6937
  Virginia:
  9401 Northeast Dr.
  Fredericksburg, VA 22408
  Telephone: (800) 634-0491
  FAX: (800) 947-8814
  http://www.hollingermetaledge.com

• **University Products, Inc.**
    517 Main St., Holyoke, MA 01041-0101
    Telephone: (800) 628-1912
    FAX: (413) 532-9281
    http://www.universityproducts.com

The Book of Discipline of the United Methodist Church is our book of
covenant for The United Methodist Church. The following references in the
Book of Discipline (relate to your task: ¶¶243, 247.5, 264, 532, 642, 1701-
1712, 2549.4. See the 2012 edition (ISBN 9781426718120).

NOTES

_____
_____
_____
_____
_____
_____
_____
_____
_____
_____
_____
_____
_____
_____
_____
_____
_____
_____
_____
_____
_____
_____
_____
_____

NOTES

_____

_____

_____

_____

_____

_____

_____

_____

_____

_____

_____

_____

_____

_____

_____

_____

_____

_____

_____

_____

_____

_____

NOTES

NOTES

_____

_____

_____

_____

_____

_____

_____

_____

_____

_____

_____

_____

_____

_____

_____

_____

_____

_____

_____

_____

_____

_____

Guidelines Resources

General Board of Church and Society, www.umc-gbcs.org, 202-488-5600; Service Center, 1-800-967-0880

General Board of Discipleship, www.gbod.org, 877-899-2780; Discipleship Resources, http://bookstore.upperroom.org, 1-800-972-0433; The Upper Room, www.upperroom.org, 1-800-972-0433

General Board of Global Ministries, umcmission.org, 1-800-862-4246 or 212-870-3600; E-mail: info@umcmission.org

General Board of Higher Education and Ministry, www.gbhem.org, 615-340-7400

General Board of Pension and Health Benefits, www.gbophb.org, 847-869-4550

General Commission on Archives and History, www.gcah.org, 973-408-3189

General Commission on Christian Unity and Interreligious Concerns, www.gccuic-umc.org, 212-749-3553

General Commission on Religion & Race, www.gcorr.org, 202-547-2271; E-mail: info@gcorr.org

General Commission on the Status & Role of Women, www.gcsrw.org, 1-800-523-8390

General Commission on United Methodist Men, www.gcumm.org, 615-340-7145

General Council on Finance and Administration, www.gcfa.org, 866-367-4232 or 615-329-3393

Office of Civic Youth-Serving Agencies/Scouting (General Commission on United Methodist Men), www.gcumm.org, 615-340-7145

The United Methodist Publishing House, www.umph.org, 615-749-6000; Curric-U-Phone, 1-800-251-8591; Cokesbury, www.cokesbury.com, 1-800-672-1789

United Methodist Communications, www.umcom.org, 615-742-5400; EcuFilm, 1-888-346-3862; InfoServ, 1-800-251-8140, E-mail: infoserv@umcom.org; *Interpreter Magazine*, www.interpretermagazine.org, 615-742-5441

United Methodist Women, www.unitedmethodistwomen.org; 212-870-3725 (membership)

Download the free training materials GUIDE TO THE GUIDELINES
and ORIENTATION WORKSHOP from www.cokesbury.com.

For additional resources, contact your Annual Conference office.